LIKE LESSER GODS

POEMS

BRUCE MCEVER

C&R Press
Conscious & Responsible

First Edition
1 2 3 4 5 6 7 8 9

Selections of up to two pages may be reproduced without permissions. To reproduce more than two pages of any one portion of this book write to C&R Press publishers John Gosslee and Andrew Sullivan.

Cover Art by Eugenia Loli
Cover Design by Lisa Williams

Library of Congress Cataloging-in-Publication Data

ISBN: 978-1-936196-70-8
LCCN: 2017943605

C&R Press
Conscious & Responsible
www.crpress.org

For special discounted bulk purchases please contact:
C&R Press sales@crpress.org

LIKE LESSER GODS

CONTENTS

III.

Special Thanks & Acknowledgements:

This book comes from the inspiration of poets I've been privileged to know and who have critiqued, edited and blessed some of the poems in this volume, principally Thomas Lux and Travis Denton, who ran and run the Poetry@Tech program. There is also the eye and nod of Stephen Dobyns, David Bottoms, Stuart Dischell, Jeffery McDaniel, and Chard deNiord, who I have worked with at Sarah Lawrence College's Summer Writers Conferences. Of course, the main thanks has to go to Travis Denton and his wife Katie Chaple who painstakingly edited and compiled this volume through several iterations. Their contributions and Katie's keen eye are the yeast and icing on this cake.

I am grateful to *Five Points*, which published "November Sunset: Maidstone Island," *Town Creek Poetry*, which published "Mystic Visit" and "Return from Georgia," and *The James Dickey Review* for printing "The Road to Nowhere," and "Memorial Day." Likewise, I am indebted to C&R Press with new management for publishing this volume.

200 Year Oak Down

With a crack through the valley
the great white oak was down
on its side like an elephant shot
by a poacher's gun,
big and greyed, its huge limbs broken
after the fall, leaves still flagging.

A south wind strengthened
this morning, attacking the old trees
who brace north—winter's early
bite at the Berkshires.

Surprising, the rot in the trunk,
termites for years undermining
its core to sawdust
that didn't show outside the grey bark,
just like her anger—slow, seething
and unspoken for seven years,
gnawed at by hard-to-notice little things.

A hard blow took down the monument
it was and the forest around it,
but in its absence,
                    there's new sky.

I.

East of Eden

The Earth for us is flat and bare.
There are no shadows.
                    —Wallace Stevens,
          The Man with the Blue Guitar

I.

It was spread before me that morning
at Utopia Farm, early April.
Soaking in a heated pool, I beheld
the twisted wolf pine, survivor
of two centuries of men
clear cutting trees here,
like the very tree of life.
It seemed all was at peace:
Having just finished our new home,
a Falling Water of local stone and timber.
A clear day, and I was off soon
for my last commute back South.

My wife and her boys en route to SFO
for their spring break while I finished
teaching in Atlanta. It seemed harmless
that I wouldn't take yet another flight
to join them while she and the kids played.
She had dinner with a love from her past
and a taste of being without me.

But an idea festered, and when
we reunited, there was no welcome.
Instead, I found her reading my diary.
She exhumed her every unhappiness,
from the past eight years, though never cited.
She told me to leave.
I slumped back to Utopia. Without her
it was hollow—a paradise gone,
all that we had built, empty.
The new house, flat—a clanging cymbal.

II.

Later, I toured an art exhibition
of artists commissioned with wandering Eden
to create fanciful serpents with legs
and ceramics of forbidden fruit.
What it must have been like
before the fiery sword barred the gate.

I had been there. But the original story
of the garden and what happened
there was wrong. In my version,
Eve seduces the serpent
and they elope with the apple—
and leave Adam (and God?)
perplexed by the tree.

I stay in the garden
and recreate the days before
her lawyer allowed no contact,
only a song to sing
of sweaty nights in her bedroom
where they crawl over vows
and our former friendship,
out into the world to wrap
themselves around and mock
the staff of healing, face-to-face,
like the twin snakes of Caduceus.

November Sunset: Maid Stone Island

A peach glow silhouettes
a pine churned by the sea's blow
like a bonsai monk
contemplating day's end,
sheltered by dunes, sculpted
by the same invisibility.

Across the narrow causeway,
over the half-iced flyway,
a late foursome ambles
off the course, joking
after a round, relishing
their fellowship.

Around the bridge, a scattering
of swans graze the waters
where they winter, look up in unison. Above,
long strings and bending Vs
of geese clamor to descend
into the peace of these tidal ponds,
ringed in cattails and reeds,
mirrored on placid waters and radiant
in gloam's half-light.

Around this small island in the middle
of it all, the village lights flicker
as they have since men came here,
and watched the day's last glory
overwhelm the unsayable absence
that fills us.

Iris

I.

As a child, I logged a whole winter
coughing in our basement apartment
near the airport, where my father
started flying for a living.

Incessant hacking haunted me
to sleep each night. My mother rubbed
menthol on my chest, blessing
and steaming all with a vaporizer.

Spring came, and one sun-filled morning,
we walked out to Ms. B's
(our landlady's) iris garden.
It was a phalanx of purple-topped stems
around a cracked birdbath
by her shingled garage—
and the coughing stopped.

It left as it had come.
I spent the rest of that morning
mesmerized by the bearded beauties
touching their petals,
pressing them to my cheeks.

II.

A month before our eighth anniversary,
my wife asked I leave her.
She wanted "space,"
affronted by a diary entry.
She would not discuss details,
nor brave counseling.
Our talks were tense
when she picked up the phone,
late evenings, or early mornings.
Then a door cracked, a civil call
and it seemed she might return
home for our anniversary.

I bought iris—blue flags,
two brilliant bunches
and put them in the living room
in a vase she'd bought.
My favorite flowers
whose velvet vulvas
invite whiffing.

I reserved a car to fetch her
and the driver mistakenly
called her cell phone,
while she was in the OR.
She told him, she would
never return—

The next weekend, returning
to our empty house,
the iris had withered
to blue knots and shriveled
in their stale water.

In coming weeks, our conversation resumed,
hope revived. She would meet that evening.
Overjoyed, I went biking in Ashley Falls
where a bridge was out
and defiantly walked my bike down
the hill and across the tracks
and back up to the road.

Through the shouts
of the construction workers,
through barriers I walked on,
determined to put
my marriage back together.

Even across bridges lawyers closed,
I celebrated my symbolic victory,
found an iris garden around a worn millstone
at the end of the road.
I stood on that stone
with my eyes skyward
and my arms outstretched
like divining rods.

Return to the City

He returns in the last seat of the Hampton Jitney,
next to his stepson, a hulking boy,
who flips the pages
of *Boo: The World's Cutest Dog.*
The youth marks the pair's progress
on an IPhone with cracked pane,
reporting the time to destination
as traffic clogs through the Mid-town tunnel.

The man in the back of the bus
relished this time when evening glories Gotham
and notches the city's canyons.
With its long days, he felt some
primordial calling with the sun
behind the resplendent towers,
syncing with old stone circles and a time far away.

The bus arcs over the Kosciuszko Bridge
while below, a city of tombstones sprawls
on both sides of the road, a vast necropolis
echoing the jagged back-lit skyline.
New Yorkers are buried like they live—crowded
contentious, elbow-to-elbow.

No matter how much he traveled
he kept coming back,
like a boxer after a pummeling,
always believing some day
he could return to his South.

Then he got a message
from his stepson beside him:
"Happy Father's Day!"
He'd never had such a note
in all his years in the Big Apple or anywhere—
the damn city had become his home.

Mother's Day

After she went into hospice,
my mother refused offers
of morphine "cocktails"
just as Jesus refused
the wine mixed with gall.
And so, I quit drinking
to feel the full tilt of my separation
because there is wisdom in this pain.

If you are lucky you see
yourself as you really are:
An overblown ego, *ME*, signifying nothing.
From this place, my mother crossed to her reward.
Jesus was resurrected to save mankind.

This is my first Mother's Day
without mother or wife.
I, too, will be changed.
Just returned warblers' songs peal
from barely green trees.

One East End

I follow the moon's path of reflection
to Roosevelt Island, where we biked last year,
through cherry trees, spilling
their petals like a pink snow,
some catching in your red hair.
In the photo I managed over your shyness,
your apartment backgrounds just across the river.

Curious, that Sunday, we came over to see
the stone church across the river
from your balcony that had intrigued you for years.
You thought it a cult, but we found it full
of spirit-filled Pentecostals who welcomed us, singing
with their smiles and flowery hats.

We managed to squeeze the most
from a day together, biking the mysteries
of this ruined island asylum,
the remains of its society that flourished
and the one re-growing here with city views.

One East End, where provisioned,
we all gathered in your living room
to ride out hurricane Sandy
whose winds shook the building.
We watched the East River lake
over the highway and spill into your basement.

One East End, where fate took you
like Cinderella to your neighbor's dinner party
who mistakenly sat you next to me.
I was glad a month later when you,
the shy doctor, emailed.

One East End, where one night
I said goodbye at your elevator
and after pecking you on the cheek,
you turned and told me squarely:

"Please know, I love you."
One East End where we slept together
with the hum of the FDR traffic
that soon became background
lulling us into sleep. Later in the night,
we'd journey with love to exhaustion.

One East End, where your first child
would have nothing to do with me,
but finally came around as his sideburns
grew, and he sprouted taller than me,
charging : "Have a good day,"
before galumphing off to school
with fluorescent sneakers.

I recall mornings best there, writing
and watching the sunrise with coffee.
(I can only see its reflection from my place.)
The red ball climbing over the north
flowing river out those high windows
through the just-greening scrub oak,
while traffic streams into Gotham.

One East End, where I was welcomed,
into your home as a traveler taken in
from the cold city and reacquainted
with the wonders of its shining towers.

But an inner child sensed something wrong,
and like foolish Parsifal, on his quest,
who stumbled into the castle of the grail,
having searched a lifetime for it,
failed to ask the crucial question,
and the castle disappeared.

Father's Day

He's behind the marble wall
of an outdoor mausoleum,
near the former Coca-Cola CEO,
all discreetly adorned and marked.

Summer's hug of humidity
wraps me and Atlanta in its hazy blanket.
Through the city's eternal tangle of traffic,
I pilgrim to my father's grave
to find a new interloper
whose family induced cemetery management
with a mini-Parthenon,
flanked by four guardian angels.
His motto's emblazoned for all to read:
Why be the best,
when you can be the very best?

I imagine this is frowned upon
by the understated local ghost crowd
at their midnight council meetings
around this park's eternal fountain.

I turned backflips to get
my father's attention, but got the back of his hand.
Eagle Scout, top of my class, Harvard grad,
started my own business,
but he didn't notice.

My late wife understood
my over-achievement obsession.
After coming close to losing her,
she had the wisdom to send me
to sit on a couch and confess my anger:
My father was a pilot's pilot
and wanted me to be the same—
to share his impoverished upbringing,
to share in his father's blessing,
who died with his family looking on
at the Sunday dinner table,
crushed from losing his business,
Nu-Grape, in a lawsuit,
and leaving them with nothing.

Mystic Visit

I stayed with old friends in Mystic
at the time blossoms litter roads
in snow-like drifts.
With first light, I was aware
of a body breathing next to me,
a warm whiteness with blond hair.

It was no dream. I was scared
to squeeze it, to lose this vision
whose ashes I'd scattered
along the river more than three
years before. But it breathed
on and was trying
to tell me something,
emanating goodness—
to make me understand.

She was gone as soon
as I thought to hold her.
No, don't leave; stay, show me
your face, tell me it's you!
She came with first light
and fled like morning birdsong.

Downstairs for coffee,
I told our friends, who ventured:
"A re-appearance."
After goodbyes, I got on the road,
and out of the shadow
of the town's scant cell service.

Messages filled my phone:
Her mother had passed last night—
she had to tell me herself
as was her way.

My car spun small whirlwinds
through the drifts.

For Our Partner

Richard Stuart Foote
May 28, 1963–April 25, 2014

It was at the time tulips
soldier-up straight and brighten
Park Avenue's corners.
In a mahogany-chaired conference room
overlooking the traffic tangle on that avenue below,
we gathered to review his deal.

With swept-back hair and a broad smile,
Richard was in fine form,
lean in a tailored blazer.
He exuded confidence.
As he explained the subtleties
of his model, you saw the path
to the gates of Golconda open wide.
It all meshed, like a Bach fugue,
the notes complex, yet ethereal
in hearing, even hum-able.

We parted, shaking hands and joking,
and Richard scootered-off to chemo,
like Jesus rode the ass's colt,
through cheers and waving palms to Calvary.

Our partner and friend, warrior-banker
we could count on,
till his Lord called him
that day of tulips.

Cows

The end of the week where I buried
a partner, like my son,
I retreated to my valley and biked
into clouds. The storm
left the field bereft with puddles
as over the horizon, thunderheads
vengeanced east.

In its wake, pairs of mallards
had taken refuge on bare field ponds.
I suspect they mate and nest there,
making families on the run.

A black cow slogged
through the mud toward
the back pasture,
her udder dragging the ground
and backside dilated.

She sought some place resembling green pasture
to drop her calf and swaddle him
like the other little angus
around the hoof-churned muddy expanse
of the birthing pen.

The mother licked the bloody afterbirth
from the foundlings—life renewed
and yellow colt's feet up
along the ditches, celebrated
with peeper chorus in the wetland—
hail the new arrivals.

Katona

I.

Escaping the city Fridays,
this is the boundary to the mythic land,
the place time forgot. Here, God
lives beyond, in his own time—
the gates to heaven announced
by lakes of swans that bunch
and graze the lake bottoms, keeping wary eyes
on anyone close to their nests.
They are the boundary guardians of Valhalla,
the Metro-North stop.

Instead of taking the train one Friday,
we drove, exiting at Katona
to find your grandparents' house,
who you said lived off their trust funds.
Filled with Picassos, Mirós, Braques—
their place you remembered fondly,
even their guard dog, with weak hind legs
who robbers killed when sacking the house.

The house, you remembered, overlooked
the long lakes below like the house
we were building together further north,
just above the confluence
of two rivers. You wanted to see it again,
knowing about where—off Reservoir Road.
We searched, but never found it.

II.

A cloudy day in April, "Tomb Sweeping Day"
for the Chinese who venerate
the graves of their ancestors,
we had to finish our service by noon
or be snarled in a swarm of traffic.

You asked me to be the celebrant
for your father's burial—in a cemetery not far
from here. He was not religious nor were you,
and I, a student at Divinity School, would do.

I researched and altered an Anglican text.
In my best suit before your family,
I calmly recited the liturgy,
commended his body to the earth
and his soul to God.

I said we had all suffered
a terrible loss, but through this pain,
we should remember, as if he were still beside us,
what your father would have us do?

I asked for comments,
and you made an elegant plea
for your family to come back together.
We tossed the ceremonial earth on the coffin
and walked arm-in-arm to our cars
just before the Chinese came
to revere their kin.

III.

Now every time I take the train to the country
and look up the hillside of graves
on that vast and statured lawn,
I think of your father and that morning
outside Valhalla—

how we honored him,
and what would he
have us do now?

Four Views of T.O.: Elegy for Thomas Oscar Allen
Mar. 12, 1939–Nov. 1, 2013

*Jesus said, "If you bring forth what is within you,
what you have will save you. If you do not have that
within you, what you do not have within you [will] destroy you.
—The Gospel of Thomas*

I.

Way back, he was the sharpest guy in the room:
Filling a tailored, pin-striped suit, sporting suspenders,
and white, folded-just-right pocket hanky.
He stood in spit-shined tasseled loafers
chewing a cigar that my wife's older sister, Suzy,
wouldn't let him smoke,
gesturing with it like a scepter as he talked.

We were fresh to the city, engaged
and living in a one bedroom on East 73rd
while Suzy and T.O. had conquered the town.
She worked on Madison for Doyle Dane;
he had risen to CEO
of a company marketing nationwide
to college kids. They hosted us
at a restaurant decorated like a Hollywood set,
initiating me with my first artichoke.

We took notes where to eat, sip whiskey,
even the name of a good dentist—
how to navigate the Big Apple's jungle
and be like them, dashing off to tennis
at Forest Hills in T.O.'s chrome-piped Excalibur.

II.

Before New York and business school,
he was an officer, a tank commander in the Marines
and led in troops who waited
on ships off the Bay of Pigs,
while we all held our breaths
with the world on the trigger of war.
He never questioned, nor whimpered,

his oath, *Semper Fi*.
He didn't speak of his time
in the Corps, but it showed through:
One afternoon, we attended a posh
cocktail party at a friend's penthouse.
Eyes turned as they entered the room,
a hush followed as they parted the hubbub
like royalty on their way to the bar.
T.O., with his scotch, settled into a nest
of socially-concerned, discussing
the city's overcrowded prisons.

T.O. listened like a sage,
tipping his drink, sizing up the crowd.
One zealous woman asked:
"What would you do about it?"
T.O. spoke last, snorting:
"I'd kill two birds with one stone;
grind them all up and feed them to the poor!"

The woman left without words,
and as if he'd pulled a pin on a grenade,
the crowd scattered to "refresh their drinks,"
leaving our wives to wonder
why we were sitting alone.

III.

National Student Marketing proved a stock scam
that had cooked its books, and T.O. ran
its only solvent unit. After the fall, he left
with a remnant and his new bride
to Tulsa to raise a family.

One Thanksgiving when Alma, our mother-in-law, invited
her daughters and their men to her Little Sandy Farm
in Good Hope, Georgia,
their boys helped our father-in-law with chores,
or rode in his buckboard while the ladies cooked.
Promptly at "harness tightening" (5PM),
we started drinking, telling stories that grew
bolder with each stiffener.
We'd take turns churning the Syllabub,
a southern whipped drink made from apple-jack brandy,
supervised by Alma's 90-year-old mother.
She determined progress with a sip
that promoted proverbs.

This year when dinner was ready,
Alma offered apologies for a hard year,
opened the silver cover to a Cornish hen
dwarfed by an oversized platter. The joke over,
she brought forth the real bird,
and we feasted with wine, then pecan pie,
topped with Syllabub.

To finish the night, we played charades,
but T.O. didn't take to parlor games
and excused himself; I followed him, tired,
to the old homestead, tracking the November frost.
Through the tall windows across the field, I saw
T.O. sitting in the glow of the warming fire
holding and turning over a shotgun.
Careful not to surprise him, I
sang and stomped up on the porch.
He told me the gun needed cleaning, put it back
in its case, and went to bed.

IV.

The last time I saw T.O. was at my mother's funeral.
Coming a couple days early, he stayed alone at Little Sandy.
After her service, he consoled me,
saying how much he savored the farm,
recalling our family's time together there.
He rushed off to catch a plane,
but confided he was "troubled lately"—
had begun prayer and meditation
seeking the peaceful places from his life,
said his favorite was Little Sandy,
and he had come to refresh his memory.
It was always the last stop
on his mental pilgrimage.
He hoped to make it back
and asked I keep this between us.

Fog of separation

fills the valley, crosses
into June, our anniversary.
It came overnight,
like a nocturnal creature feeding
the things you wish you'd done differently,
its trail clear in morning's dew.

In the east, a glow
backlights the ghost of morning,
like her "need" of space, a void
over the mountain
of your old attitudes and gripes
you must climb over to change.

The wispy curtain retreats
to circle around the mountain's base,
leaving a white halo.
Maybe she will call.
You carry your phone everywhere
not to miss its ring, perhaps
an answer to your email, your text
or one of your over-pouring letters.

Maybe say "thanks" for the flowers sent,
just to let you explain.
But the fog vanishes
to a cacophony of birds
singing up the start
of your empty summer.

The Ice Princess

The sun warmed her debut down
her clinic steps, dressed in green scrubs
for surgery, regal with long red hair,
hugging an overloaded
leather bag she toted full
of paperwork and medicine.

Though we'd been weeks apart,
she forced a smile, but didn't kiss me,
only squeezed my hand
(like my last wife before she died)
as we crossed over to the park.

We walked an oval before
the steel monolith of Sinai.
Good to see her, even if emotionless.

I'd been practicing my mercy speech
to answer the list of transgressions
she spewed on the conference call with the therapist.
My apology was on its knees before her
when she waved it off, saying
it was not my fault, she'd let it happen.

She recounted her first husband,
who she claimed tried to kill her.
She could forgive him now
because his memory
was a speck of dirt to her.

Oddly, she didn't feel anything
when her mother died,
and then got around to it—
and she couldn't feel anything for me now,
had my back no longer.

Like an Aztec priestess with my heart
raised in her surgical hands,
she chanted that her two sons, too, disliked me
along with the manny, the maid,
her sister, and not to mention, my niece.

This weekend in the Hamptons
they would have my innards for stir fry.
Still, I walked with her under
the line of elms shading 5th Avenue,
waving their greenery
like pom-poms for a game.

And seeing a sty in my eye,
she asked me in and scrambled
to the bottom of her bag,
pressed a tube of ointment
in my hand, and instructed:
"After hot compresses
put this on. Goodbye."

Funeral at Norfolk

She looked peaceful lying there
like nothing had happened, sweet
smile, red hair done plain, freckled.
She looked like a little girl
who never grew up.
Her makeup seemed invisible, no lipstick or blush,
peaceful and finally
in charge of her world.

Then, I realized I was envisioning
my wife, not viewing my neighbor's mother
(with the same name) who had passed.
Her visitation was at a parlor
in Norfolk, a place I had never seen,
but soon recognized
by everyone's trucks outside.

I took off my hat and walked
over to the family, giving my neighbors hugs.
Her former husband is a tough
farmer and mustached charmer
who plays guitar. He pulled me aside:
"What's up?" I told him
my wife had gone.

As people congregated,
there were too few chairs,
so the Mormon-preacher-turned-Quaker started
with some words about how we will all be rejoined
in the next life, particularly families.

He spoke of how Christine devoted
herself to her children almost to a fault—
would do anything to protect them
and be sure they got their lessons, despite
a rough schedule of farm work.

We caravanned to the graveside,
rock-walled and sprawling
across a hillside. Her plot
was in the back, on a knoll
defined by a stone wall.

The preacher prayed for her soul—
for its rest and journey.
He asked if anyone from the audience
wanted to speak.
Her youngest son, Ritchie, came forward.
He remembered his mother loving her
children and protecting them from their father's wrath,
seeing they had food and clothes and teaching them,
most importantly, not to hate.

He choked up and could say no more,
and I almost shared I felt
I was burying my wife—her memory—
when his brother Danny, and sister Marie
came up with their backs square
to the audience like an honor guard
of angels girding him.

II.

Return from Georgia

Leaving out in a rain storm
watering the parched red soil,
our plane climbs toward the sun.
Commuting weekly south
I have watched spring eke
from bud to full leaf.

Sun spotlights my tray table,
and a shuffle of papers where
I sometimes hide.
As we near New York,
day's end is a ball dropping into a layer
of clouds beyond Trenton.

After these years, coming back
to some temporary apartment,
always in transit from this place
to that, it was not until her rejection
that I realized this isn't home.

The great heft of the city's spired grid
is squared, with streams of red traffic west,
and white lights east, where a massive reef
of apartments define the edge
of the East River with her place
across from Roosevelt Island.
It's there the bridges span the fork
of the five waters gathering
under the Tri-borough Bridge—
a turbulent and dirty confluence.

I did not see it coming,
did not know until now,
returning from where I grew up:
The silver river snakes
into the tidal lands of Jersey
and the bulk of Staten Island
looms while Lady Liberty
illuminates on her pedestal,
torch over the harbor
welcoming me,
a migrant, home.

Memorial Day

How tall we stand and how smartly step
our phalanx of veterans, costumed
in uniforms, salvaged each year for this day.
To the boom-boom of the high school's marching band
in ice cream white and red vests, between the cheering curbs
of townfolk on Main. Our ranks thin each year,
but all services march together into a lichened city
of tombstones, homaged with flags.

My neighbor holds her husband's flying cap up—
the one he wore every year for this parade, creased by his headphones
that lucked through twenty-four flak-filled missions over Germany,
to return with his whole crew, a record.

We halt before the cemetery's central, half-mast flag.
The new preacher salves us with the 23rd Psalm,
as from memory, and a child recites the *Gettysburg Address.*
Afterwards, the names of the dead
are read with drum rolls.

The ten-gun salute rousts pigeons.
Sleeping infants and unsuspecting children sob.
Before getting back to our lakeside barbeques,
a trumpet sounding taps echoes
hauntingly from the woods beyond.

We love a parade, but few among us
would line up and shave our heads again.
Holding our entitlements like teddy bears,
we steal home.

Our Eighth Anniversary Dinner

Tradition calls for gifts
of pewter or porcelain,
the fusion of metals and firm clays
to build a strong base
for fledgling romance.

A friend directed me to a garden shop
where the owner worked in pewter bowls
and statues, but I chose a porcelain
pot of orchids, for your father's memory,
an orchid master.

Our marriage paled.
You'd thrown me out
with no good cause,
and like the Mikado, you volleyed a list
of sins stored for eight years,
amazing for its accuracy and trivia.

Surely you would keep our dinner.
Early on the morning of June 2nd,
I was in the park going
to my meditation bench
when I walked up on a robin:
An ordinary bird, but intently
focused on a patch of clover, perhaps
a helpless worm there.
He flew as I walked up,
and I found a four leaf clover
where he'd stood—the first
I'd ever found in Central Park.
You would soften, and we would
reconcile over supper.

I made reservations, but
got no response from your office,
and at five, you announced your son
had his annual physical that evening.

"Tomorrow night, I promise," you explained
and called Tuesday again at five
to leave an apologetic voicemail
that you were caught in the OR
and wouldn't be out until after nine.
Tomorrow night for sure.

I booked another table
at one of New York's finest—
the anniversary two-top in the back.
I was there early with my four leaf clover
framed for you, my omen of luck.

You were late, as always,
but called and asked I meet you
outside, to talk first.
I complied, and you walked
me across the street to a big brunette
in a rain coat on a warm evening—
a sheriff who handed me a powder blue folio
like a flattened Tiffany's box
stamped: "_____ vs. _____."
I managed, "Thank you."

You followed,
"Do you still want dinner?"
"Yes. That's why we came," I said.
And when we sat down inside,
I handed you my little handmade frame
with the clover
                I'd found that morning.

Reunion
Georgia Military Academy
Class of 1962

I.

Our class bugler Jimmy Sims,
blows taps and breaks down.
One hundred greying men, some saluting
and others with hand over heart
have come to attention around
their former bull ring, bounded
by knee-high pyramids of cannon balls.

Like a graduation procession
through heaven's gate, the chaplain,
John Brinsfield, reads the names
of departed classmates—each underscored
with a prayer-gong, struck
thirty-three times and left
to resonate into silence.

Each name surprises,
like an "incoming" round—
a memory of a camaraderie
when time didn't seem to count—
in class, on the sport or drill field,
or screwing around in refuge
from the discipline meant
to make us men.

The Commandant meted out punishment
in wasted time and shoe leather
for the pranks we played.
Before we went off to war,
we practiced here.

Unrecognizable, except by our tags,
fifty years has etched our faces.
But I can't recall the story
I saved to tell after all these years,
when it's my turn at the cocktail party.

II.

The faces of my departed mates and the story
come back with the reading of the names:
Football camp in South Georgia,
steamy August, up at dawn to run
a mile and a half around a tempting lake
we couldn't plunge in.

John Reeves, our skinny half-back,
ran in combat boots and always won;
Big Don Kirkpatrick, who caught
many a crucial pass, and our tight end,
also up-front. Duncan Dunn
star fullback, we always counted on
for yardage, coolly lagged behind.
We were state champs until Dunn
went down ramming in for the score.

With whistle in square jaw,
Franklin Brooks, our line coach,
an All-American from Georgia Tech urged us on.
For him, we would go through walls;
he made us forget the heat
and hunger for combat.

Bruised and exhausted
from two weeks of internecine combat,
pushing sleds and hitting dummies,
we were allowed one night
out to the movies. We dreamed
of something with lots of Hollywood cleavage.

We drove into Palmetto, searching
for the marquis at the Dixie Theater.
Damn!
We rubbed our eyes—
there in black and white:
"Snow White and the Seven Dwarfs."

In the Court of Fallen Lovers

We are all like cut flowers—
plaintiffs and defendants, paired
with our intercessor attorneys.
Bunched on oak benches, beneath
similar paneling halfway up
to a dull ceiling and dirty windows,
yet mercifully for us, filtering light
from the fine day outside,
which we sense to be our last—at least
never again the same or whole.

The bailiff calls the first case
and a poor fellow stands charged
by the horn-rimmed judge
not to see his girl until the court appoints "proper counsel."
He protests, assents, sits down,
and so it goes, as the black-robed judge
like the lookout raven
cawing over a corn field, reorders lives.

Around the rotunda of justice
at 60 Center Street, we're not volunteers,
but bound by legal custom, led through
this purgatory, clinging to our lawyers
like Virgil and Dante wandering
one step up from hell.

My wife and I are ushered
into chambers, the queen-bee's cell,
and charged to deliver reams
of absurd and irrelevant data,
though she has stacks on her desk,
for her worker bees come
to deposit the pollen of evidence
and make honey of our lives and assets.

Our lawyers hover and fly
at her Honor's command, busy
in the details of data digestion.
My dear wife, only now stoic, confers
with her new team, a wrinkled
veteran with unwashed hair
and his sidekick with matted locks,
central cast for the priestess of Ur.
They gloat at what they might share by thirds.
I protest over my attorney's evil eye,
sorry to still be angry
at her betrayal, but couldn't get over
my emotion in order to settle.

Settle with the woman who said she loved
my former friend from the first time
I introduced them years ago,
who now lives with him and wants me
to pay his car fare?

In these dank chambers,
above the judge's raised podium,
stacked with tottering cases
to be shuffled and re-shuffled,
over her leather back chair,
are worn words in bronze:
"In God We Trust."
It's all I can do.

Johnny
      April 13, 1943–February 28, 2014

On fame's eternal camping ground
Their silent tents are spread
And glory guards with solemn round
The bivouac of the dead.
      —Civil War Monument
      Monroe, Georgia

He was a friend who never let me down.
He once gave me his job
so my wife and I could stay in NYC,
took me to lunch with his boss
to convince him I was the man,
while he slipped back to his beloved South
to apprentice at Justice Martin's knee,
only to start his own firm,
a banker and builder of equity.

He could press his weight like an Olympian,
our Thor—once his investors sent him on a mission
to Miami to fire a gold-chained
Mafioso captain of fast boats.
John lived to tell of it, ending
the story with his feet up
on the boss's ornate desk.

Johnny was passionate intensity incarnate—
his energy rubbed off on you. He infused you with his enthusiasms,
for money-making, or money-saving,
mapped in his mind, no stranger
to intricate and intimate details
like the historic paths of blue and grey armies
he'd march his pals over.

Though continually searching
for good investments, like a setter,
he loved his family and his friends most,
through all their trials. Loyal,
he showed up for my readings;
I could spot his broad smile,
behind studious spectacles.

All this withered like a short
winter's day in Georgia,
baptized by cold rain,
worsened with ice and snow
falling into early dark.
Johnny, the man.

Like Lesser Gods

We wing south in a full plane, strapped
and bumping through heat-hazed skies.
Sudden thunderheads rise
as high as we fly to quench
an exhausted earth below.

Sun pinks the massive billows
internally pulsed and illumined
by Thor's lightning bolts. Like lesser gods
we've conquered in our age of radar,
our jet plays between the white mountains.
With this vista, my father spent his working life.

We continue south, jostled
home to Atlanta where my mother,
keeper of our family's memory,
is bedfast and can no longer
answer her phone
to tell me she has left
the keys out for me
as she always does.

The Myth

Mythologies are enormous poems...giving
some sense of the marvel, the miracle and wonder of life.
—Joseph Campbell

I'd listen to Sibelius' *Swan of Tuonela*
in our new country home
when my was wife away
working in the city. Longing,
I watched the dark
pine fronds, feather
like fans cooling a pharaoh.

The swan of this tone poem circles
the Finnish island of the dead—a lament
for the hero, tasked with killing
the black swan haunting his princess.

He is ambushed with a poisoned
arrow and drowns on the way
to fulfill his destiny.

Through his mourning mother,
he is restored. She descends
into the river of Tuonela to retrieve
his scattered body and much like Isis
gathering up Osiris,
stitches him back together.

Salved by a bee buzzing
the sad shore, she brings him life
with a drop of honey,
an elixir from the over-God's hall.

When my wife left,
my own mother's spirit
filled the void of these halls,
hewn from rock and wood,
rekindled the shimmer,
lighting the path,
                        yet unbroken.

Inn at Germantown

The first grey of morning stirs
me in a strange room, then
the birds begin their overtures.
Human kindness sleeps on,
soft beside me—the first woman
I've been with in months.
I dress and stocking-toe down
creaky stairs to a kitchen piled
with last night's dishes.

I manage to make coffee,
and wafts of the dark elixir
fill the parlor; on the wall
a romantic reproduction
of Daphnis and Chloe, scantily clad
seeking shelter from an oncoming storm.

I find milk and a veranda
that wraps this classic inn. Flags
still festoon lamp poles from Friday's parade
celebrating the town's patriots.

A will-o-wisp
fills the low field beyond
the barbecue pit at the end of the porch.
Like a leadened fog, it ebbs
and flows, played by the
breeze and sun's warming.

A meadow unveils a profusion
of daisy and black-eyed Susan—
the good ground in the sower's parable.

As there's been no word for weeks,
I'm still staggered by the last words
of my ex-wife's co-worker
who managed to call me before
going home yesterday.

She reported my ex-wife's okay,
but had taken off
her wedding ring.

The Covered Bridge at Sheffield

Over its elbow, settlers bridged the Housatonic
where it slows from its source not ninety miles north.
It adders south, cutting its course through alluvial
sand and clay, bending between stone shoulders,
like here, where it chokes narrow,
and hikers or simple-joy seekers can cross
by way of rough sawn oak beams, over banks
high enough to span spring's melt.

The river's carved its course
under the Taconic Range for centuries
while its bridgers populated cemeteries
dotting the road, shadowing it.
It blossoms with commerce now.
Coverings gave wooden structures longer life
and span, as well as charm—
today painted and postcarded.

It tempted an arsonist, who burned the bridge,
but locals since restored it,
as did a congregation who built
a church with high-arched windows
to center three crosses
on the bluff overlooking the bridge.

The church has become a bank since,
with drive-up tellers counting money
at the foot of the crosses,
just as they diced for Christ's clothes.

The stream of tourists and antique-hunters slackens
toward dusk, pulling into pubs and inns,
their neon signs beckoning,
while over and around the bridge,
the waxwings flutter, turn and spin
for their fill of the evening's flies.

Hidden Dragon

Our demons are our own limitations...
—Joseph Campbell

After a slate thunderhead grumbles
over the top of Canaan Mountain,
I bike the damp road lined
with orange daylilies to the falls.

Half-way there, I pass a sacred spring,
like one I saw in Ireland running
from the base of a tree that pilgrims
had pressed good luck coins into.
Here it's a maple, planted
as a settler's sugar bush
next to his stone cellar remains.

Its water meanders as old truths,
blessing a meadow high before haying
and colored like a Persian rug's pallet—
yellow points of buttercup, pink
from clover and cornflowers, cobalt blue.

Above the falls, swollen from rain,
the river is checked by a dam sluicing
off a turbulent channel
to a power station below.
Unable to contain the flood,
the excess torrent cascades
over the steps of stone
smoothed by the river.

I feel an ancient eye inspecting me;
out of the turmoil of muddy spill,
an awakening giant, a dragon,
his scales and plates
camouflaged in the rocks,
re-energized by the churn and boil.

Like Beowulf's last fire breather,
he guards his great hoard, and challenges me,
coming out like thunderstorms terrorizing
our valley this summer.

He's been there all along, watching
those times I've come here unawares,
but now I see the ancient serpent,
the long work, yet undone.

I've been walking around it,
many years, like a wishing tree
wanting it invisible, drinking
myself to numbness, afraid to take it on,
yet, now ready, I stare it in the eye
and go back to put on my armor.

Bev

I.

This was Bishop, hard to believe,
hunched over in his wheelchair,
drooling at the nurses station.
His eyes brightened when he saw me:
All the way from New York! he yelped
and urged me to wheel him to his room.

There, he smiled and picked up a tan cap
sporting a yellow jacket with its fist up
and put it on, jauntily askew.
On the TV was a forest of family pictures
like those in every room up and down this ward,
memories clung to during
the resident's slow slide to oblivion.

One photo was larger—
a muscular youth, a vision of Apollo
in an Emory tee at a track meet sixty years ago,
chest out, breaking the tape.

He asked about my wife. He'd married us
and I hesitated to say—
She's left me and is living with another man.

He was quiet for a long time:
Good Lord, it must hurt;
it cuts me, but don't let
this get you down—you are blessed.
He drifted away, insisting, like a true Georgian
that I have a Coke to help me heal
until his shrink came in and asked
I say my goodbyes.

Eight years ago he'd married us
to a northern crowd that still remembers
the wit of this southern bishop,
on a June day now fogging
into both our memories.

II.

He'd led the memorial service in Atlanta
when my first wife died.
After that service, needing quiet,
I sat in the empty sanctuary
and imagined Christ came off
His cross and sat with me.

Bev guided me through this grief:
It's okay to get mad with God—
tell him you're angry
and see what happens.
I did, like Job.

III.

Bishop Bevel Jones was a preacher's preacher.
My parents were among his first parishioners
of the little church he built to be big
on the edge of south Atlanta.
I got easily bored as a boy, but he kept
me and his congregation laughing,
bringing folks back, hundreds of them.

He rose to Bishop in North Carolina.
After his retirement, I'd see him
in his red brick house in Atlanta,
and his beloved wife "Tuck"
who had problems with falling;
they can no longer live together.

A Chair for him was endowed at Emory,
urgent before his dementia took hold.
He was beside me at the installation,
watching a black robed procession
file to the Cannon Chapel.

IV.

Afterwards, he'd sometimes,
as he did with his friends, call me late:
Have you heard
about the man with dementia?
and we would laugh together.

Sometimes, he'd talk me into
taking him out to an Easter week service.
Bev knew everyone at the critical time
in their lives, having married, baptized
them, or buried a relative.
Our visits took hours while
he caught up and grazed
on free sandwiches till full.

As we were leaving he asked,
Bruce, do you know why I always
wear my hat? I ventured gingerly:
Because you're bald?
No, I always keep it handy in case
I have to take up a collection.

III.

Last Walk Down 72nd in Hard Rain

My shoes and my pant legs were soaked going for cigars—
a new place complete with every brand
and a busty lighteress who smiled
when she bent over, gave a view
of her cleavage, and lit my Davidoff #2.

Someone who didn't want to talk,
but thought it right,
had visited me that afternoon
having seen my wife,
and her new lover,
who had been my friend, one I had
sympathized with since we were both widowed.
We'd corresponded, I helped him get
work, a reading at my school, found
a gig for him on St. Patrick's Day,
arranged details, let him stay
at my house, had introduced him
to my wife two years before
(she said she fell in love with him then).
He had stayed at our place
and after his readings hit
on any woman that would talk
with him, poor man, still bereaved.

I walked out in the rain—pouring
down 72nd Street, careful
as I always was not to step
on any cracks as I would break
my mother's back. I walked
past trash piles, wet dogs
in raincoats out for a piss.

Still smoking like a train on a one-thought track,
past the Theosophy Hall, the ancient
wisdom order that believes man is slowly
reincarnated to higher orders of consciousness,
but that there are some left behind.

I always stop for the enlightenment
of their windows, wondering where I would go
and where would they?
Past my plastic surgeon's
who put my face back together
after my bicycle hit and run.
I'd laid all day in the emergency room, watching
people drift from this world to the other,
holding a bloody towel to my face.
He came and slowly shot me up with Novocain,
stitched my lips and face back together
where I had eaten the street.
I came to his apartment for him
to take the stitches out.

Down to the end of 72nd, I looked out
over East River Drive to Roosevelt Island,
the illuminated reef beyond, out over
the stream of white lights going south
and red going north
to the light in her apartment window
at East End Avenue
where they were together.
I threw the butt of my Davidoff
in a cold puddle of muddy street water,
and walked on.

Concert at Opus 40

A monolith stakes the sky,
an exclamation point
of a massive Stonehenge,
measuring the mountain beyond—
distant blue in the haze,
an aloof overlord, last-lighted
by a setting sun.

Below the band is spread out
on the stone earthwork
like a platoon ready for a firefight.
Refugees and rhythms from the love-in
at not-far-away Woodstock,
the audience dances enthralled,
drawn in by the primordial beat
of tom-toms turning on libidos,
liberating picnic blankets and chairs.
The writhing crowd, taken back
to a wilder youth, now more sober,
celebrate this and life's monuments,
like the one we dance around
built by the sculptor Harvey Fite—
a man who rededicated his life
to building this massive work,
comparable to the pyramids of Yucatan,
whose carvings he studied for his sculpture
displayed here on this blue stone quarry.
He shaped this with a lifetime of stone piling,
then stepped back.
This was his masterpiece, his Opus.

Nearby, after the concert, our hostess
Harriet sits by her koi pond,
ringed by the same blue stone and calls
the circling school by their names:
Smokey Joe, Chinese Checkers,
Lemon Meringue and Mrs. Moby,
like she's auditioning carnival clowns.

Around the house, Paul's well-tended garden,
fodder for their cooking and pickling,
and an oak hangs
with druid-like offerings
of bird feeders, shading all.

We sit around the tree, talking
of the scars of former loves,
healing them with our fellowship
lasting through it all.
The mountain looms distant,
a good father listening
to our confessions.

Reclaiming Valhalla

Across the rusted steel-girded bridge
my train rumbles north out of Harlem.
It's a blue-sky morning with the trees clinging
to the last browns of autumn while some spill
yellow aprons about them.

My heart was torn out
on my anniversary eve
in this damn city, and like the hero
of legends, I was taken to heaven.
Caring Valkyries danced with me
at a Scottish-American gala
last night, their gowns flowing
like prancing winged horses.

I recall the legend says the heroes gather
in Valhalla around the hall called *Einherjar*.
There, they join Odin for final battle
with the hordes of evil
for the twilight of the gods.
In the meantime's much boasting and mead.

Before that great hall stands the golden tree, *Glasir*,
the most magnificent ever, reaching
from center of the earth clear to heaven.
Nearby, eternally nibbled by a goat and stag,
is another tree named *Læraðr*—
"the tree of betrayal," echoing Calvary.

My escorts poured malt whiskey on my wounds,
joking they were my harem and would never
leave me. I faced reality
this morning on an escape train,
the evening's drum rolls and bagpipe blare
for the highlander's honor fading
to track rumble.

Valhalla, a train stop near the end of the line,
on the way to my house, where
two magnificent trees stand, one
in front, a wolf pine, the other, an oak
supporting its raised rafters.
My God, I do live in *Einherjar*.
It's home, Utopia.

Living Waters

*Take in your hand the staff with which you struck the Nile...strike
the rock and water will come out of it, so the people may drink.*
—Exodus 17:5-7

I go back to my rebaptism in Greece.
My church group following
Paul's footsteps 2000 years later in Philippi,
along the river snaking through
the clay pits where Lydia
dyed her purple cloth
and became the first woman
he baptized.

I was moved to asked my pastor
to baptize me again while a friend
who passed two years later,
sprung to join me, to be
sprinkled with those living waters.
Beyond, I saw blue mountains
whose high springs sourced the river,
sluicing down and over ancient
aqueducts to the town.

Years later, in Saratoga Springs listening
to a young pastor's sermon on Moses
striking the rock at Horeb,
to placate his grumbling tribes,
he asked all of us gathered about him
the sign of the members of their church.

That afternoon, I biked to a valley,
the source of the bubbly
waters bearing the town's name.
There springs and geysers flowed
from multicolored rock, stained
from the mineral goodness it bears.

I walked with my friend
who was also on the trip to Philippi.
Her son and his girlfriend with their dog
came along to walk this park.
How strangely we bonded
as if a family that day,
not joined formerly, but fitting
from some time before we took
the waters of the Lethe.

Ideas gushing from the pressure
of what's right inside you—
quenching a long thirst from wandering a desert
with distrust as a companion.
I find those living waters inside me,
sourced out of hard rocks
at Saratoga, Horeb
and the mountains above Philippi.

The Bearded Man of Luther

For Ronald Frank Thiemann
Oct. 4, 1946–Nov. 29, 2012

I.

The idea came to us on an island
in the Atlantic flyway shrouded
white with snow. A distant pine—swept
and bent by the ocean blow officiated
like a priest, a big bonsai, painfully trimmed.
Here, we first talked of the gatherings.
Here, where flocks descended as if on schedule
into gloam's Gotterdammerung,
amber orange and blood red—
arrow after arrow of gangly Vs
honking and cacophonic,
coming to peace on the coastal ponds.
Grand swans circle the island
like elegant ideas.
Their graceful necks grope
the half-iced waters for sustenance.

It was in the refulgent summer,
the season that gives up its mystery
of corn and wine, when our friend
was given the bitter cup:
To learn suffering's lessons
of endurance and character, and hope
that sometimes disappoints, though
God's spirit is poured out in each of us.

II.

We saw him sit hours in pain
through a confessional first seminar
of aspirations for religious literacy
and summarize so simply and eloquently
its content; we glimpsed, for a moment,

at a promised land where he could not go.
This bearded man of Luther,
acquainted us first-hand with the Deity.
His church sent him to end the schism,
and his school sent him to salve Iran's intellectuals.
He loved his family, the Red Sox, and scholarship.
He explained the absence of God
in our public square and His troublesome
re-appearances. Shamed, but unbroken,
he stood. We took courage in his suffering,
and the hope to change the world's order.

The Poppy Lady

Moina Belle Michael
1869–1944

A blinking light slows traffic out front
of the general store in Good Hope, Georgia.
Down the road, at the place of Moina Michael's birth,
the marker says she taught school here.
But patriotism, possibly boredom,
stirred her on to New York during the Great War
to join efforts to help servicemen
transferring to and from the front.

In an empty meeting hall at Columbia,
she read "In Flanders Field."
The verses struck her with more zeal
than any revival she'd ever attended
at Bethel Baptist on Jack's Creek:
If ye break the faith
With us that die,
We shall not sleep
Though poppies grow...

She swore hearing their voices in the words
passing *her* their torch:
"In sighs of anxiety unto anguish."

Those same voices she heard
as a child walking the rows of headstones
for the Confederate dead back home
in the cemetery where she is buried.

She first saw the suasion of the red flower
as the remembrance symbol:
The salve needed for a Great War's pain.
The soldiers' blood soaking battlefields,
transformed by the war gods
into the red flowers of spring.

The Turtle in the Road

The day we were married,
after the recessional,
through the cheers of friends
and pelting rice and petals,
your son wanted to ride
with us to the reception.

The limo took the back road,
and we were high, talking about the service,
how funny the preacher had been
when the driver slammed the brakes
for a hulking snapping turtle crossing—
something from the Triassic.
Armored, she took her time
to cross the road after laying her eggs,
clomping to the safety of the swamp.

It was a sign—
mother earth's symbol:
The beast that carries the world
on her back, saying to us
go slow, consider.

Every year we have a mother turtle
cross the road from the river
to our farm's pasture and lay her eggs.
I see her sometimes close-up
in the Blackberry, ancient
and beastly, having survived
longer than we will.

The weekend after you served divorce papers
for our anniversary dinner, I biked
along our road. There was a fresh
turtle nest just dug up by a raccoon.
The feathery shells lay scattered, sucked dry.
The 'coon had scat on the nest.

Soon after your affair was dug up
I went for a walk by the wetlands
near friends, and there I saw a mother turtle,
her head just out of her nest
laying her eggs, looking at
me to say—the world goes on.

On the Island of the Smiling Loon

Afternoon rain tingles
on the cabin's pane, washing
the memory into the lake
moating the pine island.

Thunderstorms parade north
across Fern Lake as these six souls
drop off to afternoon naps
after the long drive here
and news a lost brother was safe.

Despite all efforts to forget,
betrayal pits your stomach.
You know you must forgive
or give it up to God.

Compassion sleeps beside you,
sharing her island, and somewhere
in the water lilies, a loon wails
that haunting sound, harkening

something timeworn,
going way back to the primordial—
clean living and faith,
keeping your word.

These white and black feathered birds
seek clear waters,
stand their ground
and mate for life.

The Bridge Man

       was busy with his pan and broom
sweeping up autumn's spill,
scattered like gold coins
over the Housatonic River Bridge, outside Canaan.

A true volunteer, like a Minute Man,
no one appointed him to this job.
Yet, like going to church or doing the wash,
he shows up each week to clean his bridge.

Think: How great if every citizen,
adopted a bridge, street or unloved corner
of town and cleaned it.

Maybe for him, the bridge is sacred—
his cathedral, his ticket to heaven.
Maybe authorities could sell
cleaning rights like indulgences.

Despite all my efforts for an interview,
he will not divulge his plan.
He only manages an acknowledging grunt
with a cigarette pursed
between his bearded lips, ash dangling,
yet never falling,
           as he sweeps.

Snake at My Pond

It was my former wife who saw
him first—the ugly head
mesmerizing and the thick body, striped
like an inmate, coiled,
sunning by the pond
we were about to splash into.

It was about that same time
that I introduced her to her new lover.
Instead of fessing up, she insisted
we build an expensive swimming pool—
wanted it by the end of the summer,
driving the workers to overtime.
She got wet twice, skinny-dipped, fooled me.

She's left now, but the snake's
still there eating my frogs with impunity.
The ranger came with a strapped
stick, but to no avail.
Perhaps my farmer-neighbor's
shotgun's a solution,
or maybe he will just slither
away as legend says the snakes
in Ireland did after St Patrick
chased them into the sea
pounding his snakeskin drum.

Just as We Forgive

Then Peter came and said to him, "Lord, [...] how often should I forgive? As many as seven times?"
Jesus said to him. "Not seven times, but I tell you, seventy-seven times."
                                    —Matthew 18: 21-25

After the scripture, the pastor
told his personal parable
about the love of his early life.
She had been abused by her father,
who, when found out and unable
to bear the label,
killed his daughter and his wife.

The preacher explained how
his hatred was a hook
tearing at his gut
like Prometheus' eagle
eternally dining on his liver.
It wouldn't go away.

He said his pastor helped
him write a letter to the guilty man
in prison, forgiving him,
and how that changed his life,
led him to the ministry.

When he asked us pray the Lord's Prayer
he noted its trip phrase: *Forgive us our trespasses,*
just as we forgive our trespassers.
Behind and above him,
the fanned, polished organ pipes played
aloft in the vaulted ceiling,
sun streamed through the central window
back-lighting a pine cross—
once an instrument of Roman torture
now the symbol of a god-man's victory,
the man who authored that prayer,
who forgave those driving
the nails in his hands.

God give me this courage.

What She Saw Out the Kitchen Window

For my mother-in-law, Alma Knight Black
November 20, 1918–April 25, 2003

Bare branches of winter grey
seem lucent from the lichen
thriving in Little Sandy's vale.
A strange symbiosis of algae
and fungus, it spreads with the mist,
encrusting these oak,
cedar and sweet gum.
The yard's dormant and leaf-strewn
except for green moss, gobbling
rocks and the old bricks flooring
her garden, bounded by a rusting fence
where her white-iron patio set is
still semi-circled for tea.

A trapped fly buzzes on the glass pane,
perhaps a descendant of one who pestered her.
Heraclitus was right, change
is as sure as the water coursing these shoals,
running under the great arch of the brick bridge
convicts built downstream.
But what lasts?

Here, Alma, her husband, and mother lived
with the rhythm of the land and seasons.
They retired from the city to meld
with a church community her ancestors founded.
She was no stranger to grief:
First her centennial mother,
then her husband passed,
but what overcame her was her daughter's,
my late wife's, early death.

When cancer came and she was failing,
the church's congregants came one after another,
fixed lunch, washed dishes
and wondered like me,
looking out these windows,
why, here, ordinary trees
stand so luminous?

Camellias in the Moonlight

I was up before the cold dawn
looking out the kitchen window
watching a full moon setting—
a luminous lamp turning night
into a ghost-like morning. Below,
a camellia bush bloomed full white,
its petals, vulnerable and inviting—
risking all for an early spring.

My companion gracing mild winter
days until the freeze—
this unrequited love, dressed
for a prom that didn't come.
The camellia's buds, now shriveled
are scattered in the garden
where I swept them
with a sadness hard to say.

The Road to Nowhere

Our footsteps infringe on the silence
of this place, a temple of woodland
stolen from the Cherokee,
then taken for the dam from settlers who left
their cabin chimneys like stone tree trunks.
Likewise, a telling swath of asphalt snakes nowhere
through the Great Smokeys' old growth
forest of chestnut and yellow birch,
under-storied by rhododendron and Catawba,
all toppled and cleared for this road—
appeasement for the flooded shanty towns
and ancestral burial grounds drowned
by the long lake fingers
of the TVA's Fontana Dam.

The mountain folk who raised the ruckus
saw through the government's story.
When war came, those who didn't enlist,
took minimum wage jobs
in factories with electrodes hot and hungry
to melt aluminum for fighter planes,
or ended up refining uranium
across the valley in Oak Ridge
in plants watered by the dam's power.

Our parents fought that war,
stepped up, so mornings edging spring,
we can take hikes along urgent creeks
tumbling over moss-draped boulders.

Still believing in the promise
of a country's abundant treasury,
we, unsuspecting children of a stalled economy,
keep hiking on a trail
just off the road to nowhere—
a job leading to a half-drilled cavern
dripping water from when
the funds ran out.

Reservoir at Hard Labor Creek

The new dam half-slices red clay hills,
its gleaming concrete walls balanced
in board braces raised high.
The muddy creek bleeds
through the gorge, soon closed
to build a new lake—
revenge for the drought.

I watched its progress from the beginning—
a vast valley, shorn below
its pro-forma shore line.
Bulldozers in whirls of red dust
gathered up the remnant forest into burn piles
like martyrs in a countryside coliseum.

But Hard Labor Creek?
The name tells its history: Convicts
shackled to work and each other, driven
by guards with shotguns, to build
roads and bridges here. Like mine, arching
Little Sandy Creek, stacked brick
by hand-made brick, surviving
over a century, handy work from prisoners' sweat,
wrung out of gangs here.

Looking out over the new dam,
I see my own life in reconstruction,
its course redirected
after broken vows, no remorse.
As painful as cutting off my foot
to clear my shackles, she wielded
the axe that set me free.

It woke me up to clearing
my own countryside of old habits,
re-directing roads and priorities—
threading new power lines.

A fresh bridge spans the gorge
and one more to go. I ride
to the canyon and cannot cross,
but girders reach for air, steel
and concrete will soon fill the gap.

This countryside,
like our former life together,
to be subsumed by a peaceful lake,
once woods, now cleared, charcoaled
and re-baptized by new waters.

The filling of this valley
will cover all, banishing drought,
but never tell the whole story.

Restarting the World

Under a scattering of stars, we talk
of constellations and our zodiacs aligning
since our meeting through friends.
A half-moon holds an ethereal lantern
for summary life-histories
while a soft sea breeze
encourages palms.

Relaxing in two chaises side by side,
we survey a dreamscape—
from a groomed slope to a canal, dancing
with the glittering lights of villas
on the opposite shore, only broken
by the silhouettes of sloops
hulking in the channel.

Gingerly, we go inside to light candles
in the living room and speak
of our departed beloveds. We speculate
with a kiss, hesitate, then try another.
We climb the circular
stairs to your high chamber with a ceiling
like a Mayan temple top.

Up there, a ceiling fan whorls slow,
moving the anticipation.
The Mayan's believed only a heart sacrifice
could restart a stalled world cycle,
rekindle the sacred fire. We widowers
offer ours for this cause:
Tear open our chests, spark dry tinder,
coax kindling to smoke, soon
fanned to blaze.

In the morning, downstairs,
in my guest room, I'm up early
out of a dream of having
sleepwalked heaven.

I search for my glasses
and find them on the living room table
next to some charred matchsticks
that started the whole thing.

The Roaring Fork

We bike a trail by the rain-swollen river—
muddy, boiling, and hell-bent downstream
over rocks and rills under poles of pines
reaching skyward, and the eternal aspens
quaking riverside. The stream cuts
a "v" through bedrock and swaths
down-valley. Impressive,
this power of water—the yin.

Verdant slopes reach to red peaks
patched with remnant snows
above the tree lines of Aspen's mountains.
Like noble muses they stand
over this town bustling
with the summer crowd here
for the annual Ideas Festival—
Its congregants, their world
swiftly simplified, all tagged and imbibing
inspiration from the mountains
and speakers in the tents and halls.

If only we would follow
the logic proposed here,
work together with goodwill.
But then the cancer of reality, always
intrudes once we travel home
from these summer meadows.

I try to forget the adenocarcinoma
found a week ago in my lung,
I must face when I leave this place.
But I'm together with my friend,
a lady, who brought me here,
makes me brave,
and rides beside me
into this dark valley.

For Tom

Thomas Lux
December 10, 1946–February 5, 2017

Navigating the traffic stream north
from Atlanta, the four-lane spans
the Chattahoochee shallows
where naked Yankee soldiers waded
with their clothes, packs, and rifles on their heads
to breach the city's defenses.

In the West, a peach glow announces
the opening of the gates of heaven.
I can't shake the image
of my friend, the poet writhing
from the sting of his cancer,
his mane of blond hair half-lost
to chemo. He whispers
his wishes we assure him
we will fulfill.

He lifted me up to poetry,
told me I could do it,
gave me courage when I had none.
I brought him here, down South,
changed both our lives,
can give him nothing now,
but hold his hand.

Munificent, his last words for a friend,
those gates are spread,
his blond hair restored as he strides in—
this literary conqueror from the North,
his work and words strewn behind him,
indelible and immortal:
Sweatheart, Render and that damn
Refrigerator with the Maraschinos.

Easter in Naples

We sit by the club pool for Saturday's vigil,
lunching on grouper salad and soup.
We watch children thrill
in the splash, while beyond
stretches a white line of beach,
the Gulf divided into gradients of green
like a ladder to blue heaven.

A row of palms crowning the skyline
is buzzed by a string of pelicans,
like ancient guardians challenging
a straining bi-plane's
banner proclaiming: *Poker & Racing
Tonight—Ft. Meyer's Track.*

Jesus still has temples to cleanse,
but Naples' streets with jacarandas
flowering gaudy yellow
seem far from His grim trail.
Hard to envision here along streets
lined with bougainvillea blooming magenta
and white magnolia blushes before great houses
with Spanish tiles. We have all
walked tough trails, like my wife
leaving to live with my friend,
sending me back into a grief
like the death of my first beloved.

Here everyone seems on sabbatical
from the north, escaping winters
behind high windows shaded
by air-rooted banyans.
There's no time for grief
along these placid canals nesting
boats tied in peace at their piers.
We all suffer though.

Till the old story is retold—
of the empty tomb.
My ego gutted, that was nothing
to begin with. Who was really hurt?
If these are my nail holes,
hopefully I am wiser, can
even forgive my trespassers.

I stay with a woman with a smile eternal
yet carrying a deep grief inside like mine.
Together at a sunrise service
we enter the mystery as
the sound of birds and gulls
harken the growing glow
in the east. Her hand in mine
is assuring while behind us
is the cold extinction
of a full falling moon.

Author's Notes

November Sunset: Maid Stone Island
This poem was written for and read at the Smithsonian's *First Symposium of Religion,* held in Washington DC, at the American History Museum, December 5, 2013.

For Our Partner
Richard Stuart Foote grew up in Carmel Valley, California where he was an adventurous child, but also an acolyte and Eagle Scout. He graduated from Harvard in 1985 with a degree in Economics and began his career as an investment banker at Paine Webber. That same year is when I first knew him. Richard and I occasionally worked on deals together. In one deal for Guardian Capital in Canada, Richard had to carry the initial load since my wife passed away suddenly after we began the assignment on Christmas Eve, 2000. I had complete faith it was in good hands, but unfortunately in the spring Richard's brother Ted killed himself, sending Richard into deep grief for his older brother and mentor. Richard was one of the sharpest minds in the business. He was his own worst enemy now and again, but he called on us to live with our own lion's hearts as his shone through clearly. The day he died, he gave a brilliant performance in the morning before riding off on his motor scooter, which he used to fight New York City traffic, to his chemo treatment from where he never returned. He died of a heart attack, age fifty on April 25, 2014.

Four Views of T.O.
T.O. Allan was born in New Kensington, Pennsylvania, on March 12, 1939. He graduated from Duke University in 1961 and entered the United States Marine Corps. Stationed at Camp Pendleton, he served as a tank commander, and made Captain. He was on board a ship ready to invade the Bay of Pigs during the Cuban Missile Crisis in 1962 and was discharged in December in 1964. After working for Gallo Wineries in Modesto, California, he moved to New York as president of a subsidiary of the National Student Marketing Corp. In 1971, T.O. married Suzanne Johnson (my sister-in-law) of Oak Brook, Illinois at Fifth Avenue Presbyterian Church in Manhattan and shortly moved with the company to Chicago. He was a member of Mensa and valued a good education, formal or otherwise. He loved anything with an engine, songs with great lyrics and a good beat, along with the intricacies of baseball. He was a spiffy dresser, a master at telling jokes, and a gifted storyteller.

T.O. took his own life on November 1, 2013. He is survived by Suzy, his wife of forty-two years, and sons Matthew Talbot Allan and Lucas Edward Allan.

Johnny

John Williams was born in Cordele, Georgia on April 13, 1943. He was the son of a prominent Savannah attorney, George Williams. John was a leader and athlete—president of his senior class and co-captain of the football team at Savannah High School. With a reputation for brains and brawn, he went to Georgia Tech to play football (but was injured) and pledged the Phi Delta Theta fraternity. John received a BIE from Georgia Tech in 1965 and went into the US Army where he served as a general's aid in Korea and returned to the US to complete an MBA at HBS in my class in 1969. Johnny went into investment banking in a tumultuous period with a crash in 1969 and 1974, and the elimination of fixed commissions, which sent a number of firms into mergers. He was in corporate finance at Kuhn, Loeb, Stone & Webster; Dean Witter; and Bear Sterns before getting his dream job at Robinson-Humphrey in 1986, and he gave me his job at the Corporate Finance Department of Chemical Bank. He saved my life and marriage with that move, and I was always indebted to him for it.

The Myth

The Kalevala is Finland's national epic poem and incorporates a number of characters from Finnish mythology. A main character is Leminkainen, who travels to the underworld, which is also known as Tuonela. While trying to capture or kill the Black Swan, Leminkainen is killed by an assassin's poisoned arrow. His mother begins searching to find her son and eventually learns that he's been killed. Equipped with a copper rake, she dredges the river of Tuonela for her son's body. When she finds his badly damaged body, she offers prayers to the gods and tries to sew him back together, but despite her efforts, life remains elusive until she convinces a bee to travel to see the god Ukko to bring back honey that will bring Leminkainen back to life.

Bev

L. Bevel Jones III arrived at Emory University as a sixteen-year-old freshman and went on to graduate from Emory in 1946 and from Candler School of Theology in 1949. For the next thirty-five years, he shepherded churches in LaGrange, Decatur, Athens, and Atlanta, Georgia, during turbulent times for the country and people of faith. His pastorates were characterized by intensive community, civic, and ecumenical involvement. In 1957, Jones supported what became known as "The Ministers' Manifesto," an appeal for peace during the inflammatory debate over school integration in Georgia. Along with seventy-nine other white Protestant pastors, Jones signed the document and took it to the front page of *The Atlanta Constitution*, taking a brave stand in the face of hatred. Jones says the manifesto is "an example of the kind of influence and impact that the church should have" as a force for unity. In 1984, he was elected a bishop of The United Methodist Church. His legacy of engagement continued while he served as resident bishop for the Western North Carolina Annual Conference and when he returned to Atlanta as bishop in residence at Candler School of Theology, Emory University.

The Bearded Man of Luther

Ronald F. Thiemann (1946–2012) was the Benjamin Bussey Professor of Theology and former Dean of Harvard Divinity School. Born and raised in St. Louis, Missouri, he graduated from Concordia College, Ft. Wayne, Indiana, received his M.Div. from Concordia Seminary in St. Louis, and was ordained in the Lutheran Church in 1973. He received his Ph.D. from Yale in 1976. He held honorary doctorates from Trinity Lutheran Seminary and Wabash College. Thiemann began his teaching career at Haverford College, where he held the positions of professor, Chair of the Religion Department, acting provost and acting president. As Dean of Harvard Divinity School from 1986–1999, Thiemann established the Center for the Study of Values in Public Life. In 2010, he was appointed as the North American representative to the Lutheran-Roman Catholic International Commission on Christian Unity by the Lutheran World Federation and the Vatican. Thiemann and I established the Business Across Religious Traditions (BART) initiative and the Religious Literacy Foundation. Thiemann was a leading scholar of religion and public life. His books include *Revelation and Theology: The Gospel as Narrated Promise* (Notre Dame Press, 1985); *Religion in Public Life: A Dilemma for Democracy,* (Twentieth Century Fund, 1996); and *The Humble Sublime: Secularity and the Politics of Belief* (I.B. Tauris, 2013).

Restarting the World

In Mesoamerican myth, each calendar period of fifty-two years was seen as a cycle, the end of which could spell the end of the world. Human sacrifice was used to persuade the gods (that had sacrificed themselves to start the world) not to bring the end of the present era, that of the 5th sun. Heart sacrifice was necessary for the sun to rise again and restart the world cycle.

For Tom

Thomas Lux was the Director of Poetry@TECH at Georgia Tech, as well as Bourne Chair in Poetry for nearly sixteen years. He passed away on the evening of February 5, 2017. In addition to having been on the writing faculties of the country's most prestigious M.F.A. and Creative Writing Programs (Columbia University, Boston University, University of Iowa, University of Michigan, University of Houston, and the University of California, Irvine, among others), Thomas Lux taught at Sarah Lawrence College for twenty-seven years, the last nineteen of which, he was director of its M.F.A. Program in Poetry. Lux published fourteen books of poems, most recently *To the Left of Time*, and several limited edition books that earned him, among other awards and prizes, the $100,000 Kingsley Tufts Poetry Prize, four Pushcart Prizes, and grants from the Mellon Foundation, the Guggenheim Memorial Foundation, and three fellowships from the National Endowment for the Arts. Lux was also awarded the Robert Creeley Award. He has been further honored with the Bank of New York Award for Excellence in Teaching. In 2003, Lux was awarded an Honorary Doctorate of Letters from Emerson College, Boston. Just before his death, he completed editing and writing the introduction for Bill Knott's *I Am Flying into Myself: Selected Poems 1960-2014* (Farrar, Straus, and Giroux, 2017.)

OTHER C&R PRESS TITLES

FICTION

Ivy vs. Dogg
by Brian Leung

A History of the Cat In Nine Chapters or Less
by Anis Shivani

While You Were Gone
by Sybil Baker

Spectrum
by Martin Ott

That Man in Our Lives
by Xu Xi

SHORT FICTION

Meditations on the Mother Tongue
by An Tran

The Protester Has Been Released
by Janet Sarbanes

ESSAY AND CREATIVE NONFICTION

Immigration Essays
by Sybil Baker

Je suis l'autre: Essays and Interrogations
by Kristina Marie Darling

Death of Art
by Chris Campanioni

POETRY

Negro Side of the Moon
by Early Braggs

Holdfast
by Christian Anton Gerard

Ex Domestica
by E.G. Cunningham

Collected Lies and Love Poems
by John Reed

Imagine Not Drowning
by Kelli Allen

Les Fauves
by Barbara Crooker

Tall as You are Tall Between Them
by Annie Christain

The Couple Who Fell to Earth
by Michelle Bitting

CHAPBOOKS

Heredity and Other by Sharona Muir
On Innacuracy by Joe Manning
Cuntstruck by Kate Northrop
Relief Map by Erin Bertram
Ugly Love: Notes from the Negro Side of the Moon by Early Braggs
A Hunger Called Music: A Verse History in Black Music
by Meredith Nnoka

CPSIA information can be obtained
at www.ICGtesting.com
Printed in the USA
FFOW03n1216231017
41437FF